We're Not Supposed to Tell You:
Sex Slavery, Drugs, and Other Secrets of Thailand's Prostitution Industry

by

Noi Thawattana

Copyright 2015 by Noi Thawattana
Published in 2015 in the United States of America
All rights reserved.

We're Not Supposed to Tell You

Preface

This is the book I always wanted to write. My previous book, *Thai Girl Naked*, was the beginner's-level introduction to the Thai sex industry. I kept some things out of that book, because I still needed to travel back to Thailand regularly to take care of family, and indeed I still had relatives in Bangkok. I was no longer working in the sex industry, but I didn't want the risks involved in saying what no bargirl is supposed to say.

American culture values honesty. When Americans say they want to say what's "correct," they mean something that's factually correct. Thai culture values saying what is "correct" in the moral and social sense. What's polite, what's appropriate, what's dictated as right -- and being a tattletale on Thailand's huge sex industry certainly isn't "correct."

The implications of that are more than abstract. I, and even my relatives, stood to suffer retaliation from various Thai mafias in return for saying the things in this book, the things I left out of my previous book. Now that I'm in America, together with my close family, I am no longer nervous to talk about these things.

Most Thai people associated with the sex industry know these ugly things already -- and that includes the Thai government and police, which most likely knows more about the workings of the sex industry than even I do. Some hardcore sex tourists, or perhaps men who have had long-term relationships with bargirls, may also know these things.

Just about everything I describe as happening in the Thai sex industry is against Thai law. But remember: prostitution itself is against Thai law. Depending on your interpretation, even bars are against Thai law. So, this point is very obvious to Thai people and foreigners familiar with Thailand, but many foreigners who are new to this story ask an outraged and puzzled "why doesn't the police do anything?!" As I said, the answer is obvious to Thai people, so I'm sorry to bore you if you are Thai.

But if the answer is not obvious to you, then here is the answer: the police in Thailand is a money-making organization that is interested only in money and power. They do whatever gets them money and power. That might mean enforcing the law, or ignoring the law, or using the law to shake down certain people, or any number of things. The law is just a tool they can use to make money. And while I know that in America, being a policeman is considered a somewhat humble job, in Thailand, being a policeman is like being a gangster: a somewhat glamorous and tough road to riches.

There's a whole big story to be told about the Thai government and corruption. That's beyond this book, because I'm not a lawyer or a historian, only a former bargirl who wants to be a journalist, and I'm not the best person to tell the broader story of Thai corruption. We Thai people strongly believe in "only do the job for which you're suited," and I'm suited to tell you the insides of the sex industry, but I don't have anything to say about the Thai government that couldn't be said much better by many other people.

We're not into it: the Hollywood game

There's a story out there that we're enjoying our lives as bargirls or prostitutes, and we do this job because we like to have sex, or like sex for fun. That is a view held not only by foreigners, but also by most middle and upper class Thai people.

In the case of Westerners, the view often comes from what bargirls tell them. Every bargirl says she loves her job, because what fun is it having sex with a girl who tells you that she hates what she's doing? (Ok, some guys do get off on that.) And what she says changes only when there's a serious prospect of the man wanting to marry and "rescue" her, at which point she exaggerates about how much she hates her job.

For Thai people, there's a belief that we are meant for this job, because we're just low-class working people, or we did something in our past lives to deserve this job, or, most likely, that we are doing this job because we're lazy and horny, and what better job for a lazy and horny girl than being a bargirl?

I never had an orgasm with a customer. A few of my friends did, but only when it was a long-term customer who became almost like a boyfriend to them. And I always despised my job. Although, to be fair, I would have also despised any other job that was available to me, such as working in my parents' restaurant or being a data entry clerk or a shop girl.

Every man wants to feel like a sexual superman. Every man wants to feel special. Thai bargirls aren't stupid, despite what you may think. One of the things we teach each other, one of the most important things we teach each other, is how to fake sexual enjoyment and orgasm.

Bargirls and all kinds of Thai prostitutes are known to play a game called Hollywood. They get into a lesbian kind of position with another, more experienced girl. And girl 1 (experienced teacher) pretends to be the male customer, while girl 2 (student) pretends to be enjoying it. Girl 1 coaches Girl 2 on how to fake an orgasm, including not just what to say and how to moan and how to hold her head, but how to contract her muscles, including her vaginal muscles, to fake an orgasm. She will put her finger in the other girl's vagina to test how well she's faking the orgasm. This is all training. Hollywood.

I was introduced to Hollywood on slow nights when I worked on Soi Cowboy. Sometimes when we were getting ready and putting on makeup together, two girls would do a Hollywood show for the other girls, with the other girls being usually amused and maybe a little bit aroused by the sight of the huge fake orgasm. And if you've seen the "lesbian shows" in the foreigner oriented bars, they're just the bar owner's attempt to cash in on the games of Hollywood that they've seen.

We guess that Western girls aren't very good at pretending to have orgasms, because foreign customers are so sure that our orgasms are real, because we clutch our legs around them or we clench our vaginal muscles or our mouths quiver or something like that. Step it up, foreign girls! That's basic stuff we learn at Hollywood.

Now what about the other stuff, the romance, or at least the going out with customers? I had one friend at Soi Cowboy, another coyote girl, named Nui, and she absolutely hated having to go on dates with customers. She preferred just to have sex and get it over with. Her least favorite customers were the long-term expats, since they usually spoke some Thai, and had a lot of free time -- so they invariably insisted to take her out to a club, see a movie, have dinner, and so on and so on, before the sex act.

The guy is having a great time. He does what he wants, and has a pretty girl on his arm. The girl is bored out of her mind. She has to be out doing things she finds absolutely boring, and pretend to be enthralled. She usually has to eat food she doesn't like and pretend it's delicious and drink alcoholic drinks she doesn't like and say they're wonderful, and so on, as a prelude to having sex with a guy she thinks is disgusting and say he's a stud.

And she is paraded around as an obvious bargirl, in Thai people's eyes. The foreigner of course treats her like a girlfriend or like a princess or like a wife -- that doesn't make her look any less like a prostitute in Thais' eyes, because we Thais know that foreign guys like to treat bargirls like princesses. She says, of course, she is proud to be seen with a foreigner, but the reality is, she is ashamed to be seen as the bargirl she most obviously is.

Most cruel is the snide rude treatment and "micro-aggressions" such a bargirl gets whenever going out with a guy. There's nothing big enough to complain about. But when a foreign guy takes a bargirl to a fancy restaurant, she is miserable not only because the whole setting is uncomfortable and the food is disgusting and the company is boring, but also because she knows exactly what the customers and waitresses are saying -- "look at that hooker."

A hostess or massage girl going out with a Thai customer? Also uncomfortable. First off, hostess and massage girls are often forbidden from seeing customers outside of work -- sure, it happens, but the boss won't be happy -- so we preferred to meet the customers directly at their homes, or in hotel rooms, as I usually with met my hostess-bar boyfriend Aek. But second off, Thai guys, even more than Western guys, expect girls to drink a lot when they go out, maybe to make them more pliable to sex. That's never comfortable. And Thai guys, more than Western guys, expect girls out with them to always look perfect, act perfect, have a tiny girly voice, and so on and so on -- which gets tiring if we're doing this after spending all day acting with customers and before a night of faking orgasms with this guy in bed.

So which is better, Thai guys or Western guys? If they're customers, whatever, whichever one pays more. Rich Thai guys tend to be the best in paying and tipping, followed by Western guys, followed by non-rich Thai guys. The problem with non-rich Thai guys is that going to a hostess bar or a brothel is a big expenditure for them, and they have the mentality of "I'm blowing a week's pay on this, so I'm going to get the absolutely most possible." Which is not a bad mentality for a food buffet, but we working girls don't really like it.

Have you heard of bargirls saying Thai guys are all violent drunks? Mostly that's what she says as part of the Hollywood act for you. If you were a Thai guy, she'd tell you all Western guys are violent drunks. But a little bit of that is that the Thai guys who would date a hooker are in fact often violent drunks, while Western guys of all kinds of types would date a Thai bargirl.

Either way, if it's paid sex, or a paid outing, we're not enjoying it, other than enjoying the money we're making. And if a girl tells you she loves being with you so much, whether sex or going out, that she'll have sex with you or go out with you for free? It just means she has another way to get money from you. It might be an expensive meal for her and her friends, or a shopping trip, or a sob story about a medical bill. Or it might be the famous game of telling a man you love him for him and you only want to spend time with him and you don't want any of his money and you'll even pay for dinner -- Western guys love this, telling the story of how the bargirl paid for dinner -- of course planning for the bigger setup of getting this guy to marry you and take you to his country.

Thai girls aren't bad people for doing these tricks to try to make more money. Remember, the situation where you meet them, you are paying them money for their companionship and their body. Why is it so bad if they find other ways to charge you money for their companionship and their body? In any case, it's really, really, just a business.

Here in America I met a Thai girl who never worked in the sex industry in Thailand, then met an American man, moved to America with him, and he ended up being an abusive drunk. She got her green card, then divorced him, and because she had a great body but no education or job skills, she became a stripper. She told me that what she finds amazing about American men in the strip club is that they all really genuinely believe the stripper likes them and is sexually aroused by them; she never worked in sex in Thailand, but in her opinion, Thai men are more cognizant of the Hollywood aspect of prostitution.

The golden handcuffs

Westerners have two serious misconceptions about slavery in the Thai sex industry. The first misconception causes them to overestimate how much slavery there is in the Thai sex trade. Unfortunately, the second misconception causes them to seriously underestimate it.

The first big misconception is that sex slavery is everywhere in the Thai sex industry, and that every Thai prostitute is physically chained to a bed where she must service twenty clients every night, or some such thing. Usually this misconception comes from well-meaning women's magazines or charity groups who want to end the evils of prostitution. Their concern is commendable, but their facts are wrong. Such situations of physical imprisonment do happen, but they are rare. Being rare doesn't make them acceptable, but they are rare. And they happen more often with non-Thai women than with Thai women working in Thailand.

Non-Thai women are sometimes subjected to physical restraint and regular physical violence, especially in low-profile, unmarked profiles that might also traffic in children. It's true, but it's a tiny picture of the situation. And accusing any Western man who goes to Thailand for bargirls of having sex with physically chained-up sex slaves is a gross exaggeration. The women Westerners encounter in the bars of Bangkok are almost always Thai, and are almost never subject to physical restraint or regular physical violence.

What, there are non-Thai women working in prostitution Thailand? Sure, why not. They're not American or Australian or Swiss. They are sometimes from the former Soviet Union, but most commonly, they are from the poorer countries that border Thailand, especially Laos, Myanmar, and Cambodia. In either case, they are usually from ethnic minorities in their countries, and are almost as out-of-place in their home countries as they are in Thailand. Their situations in Thailand are pretty terrible, but the situations they're leaving in their home countries are also pretty terrible. (By the way, this is outside the scope of this book, but Thai women in prostitution outside of Thailand, especially in Asia, are almost always debt slaves.)

The second misconception, equally wrong, is that if a girl is happily dancing on a stage and goes out drinking and dancing with you, she is not in slavery. The second misconception is related to the first one, of course, that equates modern Thai sex slavery with something like the black people's slavery that Americans are familiar with. Westerners tend to take things at face value. If she tells you that she loves working in a bar, it's true. If she tells you no one is forcing her, it's true. If she tells you she does the job for fun, it's true. And if there are no physical handcuffs or shackles on her, then she's not in slavery.

And according to this belief, many Western sex tourists are absolutely sure, and will tell you with great certainty, that there is no sex slavery in Thailand, or that there is no sex slavery in the sex venues they visited in Thailand. They don't say "I didn't see any evidence of it, but it could exist." Nope, they say, "I know for sure, there are no sex slaves there! These girls happily go out drinking and dancing with customers!" Foreigners usually not only don't know what's happening, but also don't know what they don't know. I could understand them coming to Thailand and saying, "I have no idea what's going on in these places!" But going around saying that they're sure of how things work is flat out wrong and ridiculous. (But then, who knows... maybe I sound the same when I make comments about America...)

Sex slavery is everywhere in the Thai sex industry, often among the same girls who are happily going out drinking and dancing with tourists. It doesn't involve being constantly physically chained to a bar. It doesn't involve daily beatings. But there are definitely restrictions on movement. And there is definitely a big threat of physical violence, to both the girl and her parents, if she steps out of line. Physical violence doesn't need to happen constantly, in front of customers, for it to be a very real part of what's happening. It's always in the background.

Bosses in Thailand don't keep slaves without reason. It's always related to, and justified by, debts. These debts can be from actual cash that was given to the girl, or from payment for gambling, or for "compensation" demanded from the family from some perceived transgression, or, often in the case of women who aren't Thai, completely made-up debts that the girl never agreed to.

Cash and gambling debts are easier to understand, but "compensation money" and completely made-up debts are a little bit more difficult to understand. Compensation money is like an American lawsuit judgment, except decided by the mafia or sometimes by the village or by a village bigshot -- and can be for something that in America would never get any compensation, even in the most lawsuit hungry personal injury lawyer's mind.

For example, if a bigshot decides that a poor person gravely insulted his family, he demands compensation from that poor person. "Gravely insulted" could, for example, mean reporting a rich person's crime to the police, or not giving a rich person whatever they want (land), or, in the case of having teenage children, a poor person letting their teenage son get anywhere near a rich person's teenage daughter. All those are grave offenses in Thailand's unwritten law, which is what runs the country, even if there is nothing about them in Thailand's written law. And any of those can lead to it being decided that the poor person owes some large amount of money to the rich person.

Compensation can also be sought for things that are more usual for Americans -- for example, if you injured someone in a car accident. But your ability to pursue compensation is solely dependent on your social standing and your ability to get gangsters and policemen on your side. And because poor people seldom have cash to pay immediately, your ability to collect compensation over time is solely dependent on the connections you have to make sure that person pays up. Cases of rich people having to compensate poor people are very rare, unless that rich person is trying to make Buddhist merit, or unless that poor person has someone intervening on his behalf (a monk or a celebrity or another rich person).

Completely made-up debts are common for women not from Thailand. The women from other places really have no recourse of any kind. They don't have any family or connections in Thailand, they might not speak the language well, and in general, Thai people will not help people from "lower races." (Such as Burmese, Laotian, Cambodian, Vietnamese.) And they have no legal immigration papers in Thailand. Unlike in America, where even if you don't have any immigration papers you are still deserving of police protection, in Thailand if you don't have immigration papers, no one will help you.

You can see this in recent news about the Rohingya refugees from Myanmar trying to come to Thailand. They are enslaved, exploited, or sent out to sea to die. However little a Thai policeman or government official cares about the average Thai person, he cares even less about an average "lower race" person. Two reporters in Phuket were recently put on trial for talking about the Thai Navy's involvement in human trafficking of Burmese refugees. That is one of the very few times anyone would speak out. But abuse of refugees and workers from Southeast Asia happens all the time in Thailand, and whatever small reluctance a Thai government official might have about pushing a boat of Thai people out to sea to die, they don't have any such reluctance about non-Thai "lower race" people. I'm sorry if I sound angry about it, because I am angry about it, and I'm glad to live in America now. I will always love Thailand, but some things about it I can't accept.

The foreign women's problem is that they never know the situation awaiting them before they come to Thailand. Most often in their country they're told that there's great, high-paying work in Thailand, and a visa is ready for them -- and when they arrive in Thailand, they're presented with "this is the debt you owe us for bringing you here," which they never agreed to, but there's literally nothing they can do about it, and they're told to work in the sex industry to pay off the debt. And of course if they try to pay off the debt, who knows how honest the pimp's accounting is? Most often, by design, they are stuck in their situations for the rest of their lives. When they are too old for prostitution, they are moved to be cooks or maids, earning even less money, and in an even more hopeless situation. Those who manage to escape back to their home countries come back with nothing -- not the big bags of money they were promised when it all began -- and they and their families live in constant fear of retaliation from gangsters.

Next we can talk about cash debts, family-related debts, and gambling debts. But first, something important to explain about debts in Thailand. In Thailand, if your parents borrow money from the mafia, and then they disappear or die, the debt doesn't disappear or die along with them; the debt gets passed on to whoever is most likely to pay it, usually the next-of-kin, but it can even be a close friend or associate who is not blood-related. If you borrow money from the mafia and then you disappear, if the mafia can't find your family, your best friend gets the debt, even if they didn't even know that you had the debt. It often happens that someone's life is ruined -- or turned into a chase of paying down a debt -- because a relative walked out on a debt and the mafia went after the next of kin. "But that's not fair." Right, maybe it's not fair, but the mafia does whatever is necessary, and in Thai culture, it is indeed fair -- in Thai culture, you *are* your family and your close friends, so it only makes sense that your family and close friends are liable for your debts.

Almost all sex slavery in Thailand involves the parent-child relationship. Most commonly, parents, in rural Thailand or in the countries bordering Thailand, need a lump sum of money, often for an unexpected emergency such as a failed crop or a natural disaster or a bad night out gambling. There are local gangsters in every Thai village who are known as loan brokers, and they lend money, based on the daughter as collateral. The daughter is expected to work off the debt. And if it's not paid off, both daughter and parents and all the family are in severe physical danger.

The other way it involves the parent-child relationship is that sometimes it's the daughter who borrows money from the mafia. The parents' and siblings' physical safety, in addition to the daughter's, is the collateral. The mafia has its web of informers -- most importantly, bar owners, as well as the police officers who patrol the bar areas -- but in case a girl just disappears (often going to a foreign country with a customer), it's the parents and grandparents who are on the hook for the debt. The girl's parents and grandparents most often live on farms and aren't very mobile. And if a girl has neither literal collateral, nor parents who live in a fixed place on a farm, the mafia is unlikely to lend to her.

Bar bosses are not only facilitators in this game. They are active pushers to make it happen. They profit all around from these debts. They often actively encourage borrowing money in this way, especially knowing the girls' soft spots, such as their families.

"Don't you think your younger brother deserves to go to university?"

"Don't you think your father deserves a new motorcycle?"

And so on. The bar bosses can be the lenders, or the bar bosses cooperate with mafia lenders, who pay the bar bosses a commission for any loans they bring in. Either way, the bar bosses win, because a girl in debt is less of a worry. Normally one of the costs of running a bar is staff recruitment and turnover. This was less true when I was working in the business a few years ago, but nowadays, there are so many decent (well, comparatively decent) jobs available for less educated Thai women that bars are no longer the only game in town, and staff retention and recruitment are major business expenses and problems for a bar owner. A bar is like any other business. And while traditional long-term employment contracts would be unworkable and unenforceable, mafia debt contracts provide a convenient way for bars to keep their staff.

The usual definition of "debt slavery" or "sex slavery" used by the international organizations is a debt that includes a specific method of being paid off, and that is enforced by threats of physical violence. Thai prostitutes' debts fit this definition perfectly. The slight exception is that the girl can change bars or venues for paying off the debt, but only with the lenders' approval, and of course also having a "transfer fee" (usually about 5%-10%) added to her debt. She is unlikely to receive approval for transfering to a brothel or other venue that might make her more likely to run away from the debt.

One common way to encourage a debt contract to be created is a pimp (meaning any owner of a prostitution establishment, such as a bar or massage shop, or just a street pimp) cooperates with a plastic surgeon. And they pressure girls to have plastic surgery, usually breast enlargement surgery, in return for a loan, of course a loan that's designed to keep the girl chained to the shop for a long time. This exists for non-prostitutes too; plastic surgeons cooperate with all kinds of shady lenders to try to get poor women into big debts.

The plastic surgery offer is also made to girls already in debt, when the pimp has a hunch that the girl actually has a chance of paying off the debt and no longer racking up interest charges and housing fees and whatever and staying chained to the shop. She is told that she should have plastic surgery, usually the bigger breasts, so that she is more attractive to customers and can pay off her debt faster. Which is a lie. Of course the cost is high and it's meant to keep her in debt.

If a bargirl in a foreigner-oriented prostitution venue has obvious breast implants or other plastic surgery, it's possible that the plastic surgery was paid for by a boyfriend or financial sponsor, or even that she's old enough to have saved up the money herself for the surgery. But if you see a young prostitute in a Thai-oriented prostitution venue (like Ratchadapisek Road places) with breast implants or other surgery, you can be pretty much 100% certain that the breast surgery is from a debt contract.

I remember my acquaintance Nit from the hostess club where I worked. Nit was born on the Burmese side of the Thailand-Myanmar (Burma) border; her family is ethnically Chinese and spoke Burmese and Cantonese at home, and she also had a Burmese name and a Chinese name, and a Myanmar passport. It was commonly known in her village that anyone who didn't want to stay home in the hopeless village would get a Thai "arrangement," and be smuggled into the Thai side of the border.

Actually in the border areas near Thailand, sometimes these "arrangements" are made when the girl is very young, much too young for any kind of work. A Thai gangster makes a down payment on the girl, say about $500 USD, and then promises the family another payment, maybe $5,000 or $10,000 USD, depending on the family's bargaining skills, when he finally comes back to take the girl to work.

As far as the parents know, the payment is a bonus, and the gangster is going to provide the girl with a good job and a good life in Bangkok. They usually don't really consider that they've sold their daughter into slavery. They think they've just gotten her a job for when she's older.

There's a false belief that it's the poorest of the poor parents who sell their daughters in this way. Actually, the poorest of the poor are most often happy just scraping by. They often don't have any big-city needs or aspirations. It's those the next rung up (pretty much my own family background), the "working class" who aren't desperately poor, often have dreams of bigger things, and also often have debts to pay off or needs for cash for a motorbike or whatever.

Nit was actually first taken to a Chinese restaurant in Chiang Mai, where she worked as a cook and waitress (she knew Chinese cooking from her family), but the bosses said she owed one million baht (about $30,000), and they were paying her $200 a month in the restaurant and deducting various "expenses" such as housing and food, so she was left with something like $50 a month to live on and to pay off a $30,000 debt. The situation was actually set up for failure. They knew she wouldn't be able to pay off the debt. That was the point.

They offered her to go to Bangkok to work in a "massage parlor" (a brothel) on Ratchadapisek Road, one serving almost exclusively Thai men. But if she wanted to take that opportunity, she had to go into debt for an additional 500,000 baht, for "job transfer costs" and also for the breast enlargement plastic surgery. Nit is a small framed, short, thin girl, very cute. She didn't really want the breast enlargement surgery, but she went along with the idea.

When Nit woke up in the hospital in Bangkok and felt her new oversize fake breasts, she cried. They were hard and unnatural and felt terrible and, to her eye, look terrible, totally off on her girlishy small body. And, as she knew, she was heavily in debt for them. She couldn't get rid of the breasts, nor of the debt. She actually considered going farther into debt to have the implants removed, but she realized that it would leave scars that would make her unmarketable in prostitution, and would make it impossible for her to pay off the even bigger debt. Those breasts are the thing she regretted most in her life when I met her as a co-worker in the hostess club -- and I knew the breasts story well, because she told it to all of her coworkers, sometimes multiple times, expressing (in her Burmese and Chinese accented Thai) exactly how bad of a deal they were for her.

Fortunately for her, after three years of working at the Ratchadapisek massage parlor, she paid off the debt, with some help from a customer from Hong Kong who donated some money to her cause (as she told him she had a debt to pay off before she could get her passport back and travel to Hong Kong with him) -- and she steadfastly refused her massage bosses' offers to go into more debt for this or that. She knew better than that. She actually managed to get out of debt, had a few Hong Kong and Singaporean boyfriends, and when I knew her, was doing ok working at the hostess club. She still had the breasts, and knew they were moneymakers in the hostess club, so she grudgingly kept them. I wasn't so bold as to ask about her immigration status in Thailand, but I assumed she had made enough money to buy some kind kind of document.

When a girl like Nit, who is paying off a debt, is working at a brothel ("massage parlor") to pay off her mafia debt, she doesn't keep any of the fees paid by customers for her services. Normally in the Ratchadapisek massage parlors, girls get about half of the total fee for themselves, with deductions for things like room cleaning and laundry and uniforms and sleeping quarters and whatever else the boss can think of. Sometimes if the customer gets a "free drink" at the massage parlor, it is actually charged to the girl's account. But in the case of a girl who is working off a debt, she doesn't get any cash, and any "deductions" are charged to her debt -- with the boss's goal being preventing that debt from diminishing. Girls are also made to hand over any cash tips to the bosses, to go toward their debts. They usually do hand them over, because they do want to pay off their debts, and also because the bosses like to make violent physical examples of any girls who break the rules by keeping cash tips. In the case of Thai girls, a girl might be able to go through the process of claiming that her documents were lost, and pay a hefty bribe (where would she get the money?) to have them replaced, but it's also likely that the debt mafia would have informants inside the passport and ID card offices. In the case of a non-Thai-citizen such as Nit, she was a Burmese citizen, and even though a Burmese passport wouldn't do her much good in Thailand, it would still be extremely difficult to procure.

In Western tourists' image, a slave would have to be physically restrained on the premises in order to be slaves. Instead, bosses keep all the girl's identity documents -- their passport and ID card and perhaps birth certificate -- so that the girl can not go to hotels with customers (a hotel usually wants to see a prostitute's ID) and cannot do anything like leave the country or get an apartment or get a new job, all of which require presenting your original identity documents. That is as good as physical restraint.

Nit was an unusual case because she got out of the debt slavery. Most prostitutes in Thailand never get out of it. That's by design. It's like the credit cards in America that keep sending you cash advance checks, hoping you take yourself deeper into debt.

As I mentioned, in many cases the debts are incurred not by girls, but by girls' parents. There are many cases of actual debts, often for vehicles or for bad crops or for gambling debts, taken on by parents and passed on to their daughters. And you know, in Thai culture, especially upcountry Thai culture, daughters are like farm animals, beasts of burden. The result of that is that not only actual one-time mafia debts are passed to the daughters, but also the continuing family obligations. A daughter who is working in the prostitution industry becomes a beast of burden for a whole family, and there's no way to stop it, because the bills and the needs just keep coming.

Those girls who aren't slaves to debt to mafia organizations are slaves to the financial needs of their families. Many times, the distinction is very blurry between the two. A girl might have to send 20,000 baht every month to her parents, and her parents use that money to pay off a mafia debt. Everybody knows that if the parents don't pay, the mafia will go after the parents and the girl. Most likely, the mafia is in contact with the girl's bar boss, to keep tabs on where she goes. Now, is this girl a debt slave? Maybe, maybe not, but to her, it sure feels like it. But remember that Thai girls are brought up to believe that Buddhist past lives put them where they are, and if they bear their burden in this life, then they will have an easier time in a future life.

If there's no mafia or family pressure grabbing the girl's income, there might be a drug addiction. Many girls in prostitution -- although fewer in foreigner-oriented prostitution -- are addicted to methamphetamines, in Thai called "ya ba," or "crazy medicine." It helps them stay up late and stay thin.

There are also gambling habits. Bangkok prostitutes usually are not from Bangkok (I was an exception), and they live together in group apartments around the Ramkhamhaeng area. And what do they do when they have free time? They gamble! They can gamble on anything, but the most common gambling game by far is *pok deng*, which is like Thai blackjack, always played by a circle of friends, and, unlike Western blackjack, played almost always by women. I know that nowadays, girls often play pok deng using phone apps, but a few years ago when I was working in the business, you always saw decks of cards wherever hostess or massage or bar girls gathered.

Girls with no debt contract, no family in constant need of money, and no bad habits are highly desirable -- as girlfriends by shady guys. They are sometimes called "fat chickens" in Thai. "Chicken" ("gai") is Thai slang for a prostitute, and a fat chicken is a prostitute with a lot of money. Keep in mind that no decent Thai guy would want a prostitute as his real girlfriend or wife (maybe as only a side sex buddy). But a not-so-decent guy, usually an unemployed playboy quite a bit younger than she is, loves to find a prostitute who is making good money. He keeps her hooked on him through something like emotional addiction, although he might also physically beat her or encourage her to become a drug addict. But most commonly, he gives her the love (or "love") she is sure she is missing from her life, and reinforces the idea that no one else will love her except him.

These "boyfriends" are also kind of like pimps, and in the case of girls who are walking on the streets and not employed by an established massage parlor or bar, they really function like the pimps you know in America, maybe standing by and providing physical protection to the girls. In the case of foreigner oriented prostitution, the boyfriend/pimp might be something like a "taxi driver" or "tour guide" or "travel agent" who tries to extract additional money from the foreign customers. He can also pose as the girl's "brother," a "brother" who always has some kind of serious medical condition, which of course needs a lot of money to cure.

Are the girls slaves to these boyfriends or relatives? Effectively, pretty much, yes. There is not only the threat of physical violence, but the threat of social shame. In Thailand, unlike the case in the Western world, your entire self, your entire being, is your social reputation. You can't "ignore the haters." Public opinion *is* your identity. And a girl who is seen as disloyal to her parents is more or less automatically ruined in Thai public opinion. (Disloyal to her foreigner boyfriend or husband? Not really a big deal.)

Alcohol, meth, and other vitamins

Hostess-club girls have bad relationships with alcohol. Some are alcoholics to some degree, and start drinking every day before work even starts, then eagerly down every drink a customer buys them. You can usually identify them as the girls who request real liquor in the drinks that customers buy them, instead of having the bartender mix in some colored water to keep the customers happy. Most, however, dislike the amount of alcohol in their lives, to the extent that they'd likely rather have sex with a strange man than drink the drink he's just bought them. They don't dislike alcohol. But they dislike the huge quantities they're expected to consume if in one night they have many customers buying them a few drinks -- especially if those customers do the douchey thing of sniffing or tasting the drinks to *make sure* that there is really alcohol in them!

Bargirls are in a better situation with alcohol than hostess club girls are, because they're expected to be dancing on stage, and go home with a customer, rather than just sitting with a customer and downing drink after drink after drink. If bargirls fall into alcohol problems, it's usually after they've married a foreigner and are no longer working in a bar, and perhaps no longer meeting their friends. They often don't know what to do with themselves, and fall into drinking.

Alcohol is popular with Thai women less than with Thai men. But drugs, especially yaba (methamphetamines, sometimes mixed with caffeine and sweet flavorings), are absolutely rife in the Thai sex industry.

Yaba means "crazy medicine" in Thai. It used to be called "yama," "horse medicine," because it was used as a stimulant to make horses work harder. As it became more popular among humans than among horses, it became called yaba, because of how crazy it makes its users.

It is usually sold in multi-colored pills and can be swallowed or placed under the tongue, but most bargirls smoke it from aluminum foil pipes. I would guess that maybe 80% of bargirls are occasional users of yaba. Before Thaksin's war on drugs in 2003, bargirls smoked yaba pretty openly, but after 2003, they only do it behind closed doors. As with many things in Thailand, the law doesn't dissuade people from doing something; it only makes them more careful about hiding it. Bargirls don't like yaba any less now than they did back then. In fact, it's probably even more popular than it used to be. Yaba gives them the three things bargirls want: emotional numbness, weight loss, and late-night energy. There is a sticky-sweet-chemical smell around when yaba is being smoked. I had sometimes smelled that same smell even before I worked in the sex industry, but I didn't know what it was until I arrived on Soi Cowboy and saw groups of girls huddled around before working hours smoking this sweet stuff out of foil. No, I never smoked it myself, because I'm always very scared of any drugs (even cold tablets). But it's common among bargirls in the foreigner areas, and even more common among prostitutes catering for Thai men.

Remember that in the prostitution scene for Thai men, being skinny is paramount. And what foreign men can accept as "slim," Thai men might dismiss as "fat cow." There's also the fact that Thai pimps want girls to be addicted to yaba. Not only do they work longer and not only are they less in control of things, but they always need money. One yaba pill costs about 500 baht, and the serious addicts need one pill every few hours; you can imagine how profitable this might become for a pimp, who is usually also the drug dealer.

I know that in American culture, drugs are drugs, and medicine is medicine, and the two don't really mix. You buy illicit drugs from a guy on the street, and you buy pharmaceuticals from a doctor or pharmacy. But in Thailand, drugs, as many things, are much more of a gray area. While we do have doctors in Thailand, many people find them too expensive or untrustworthy, and most sickness is addressed by going to a local "medicine man" kind of figure -- like a pharmacist, but more like an herbalist and a drug dealer in one. The things sold by this kind of figure often do make you feel good, and they're often in some gray areas between pharmaceuticals or illegal drugs. They're euphemistically called "vitamins" by Thai people.

It is not unusual for the medicines from this kind of traditional pharmacist to include methamphetamine, heroin, cocaine, or ecstasy -- they do make sick people feel better, and they encourage repeat business. Many terminally ill Thai people are unknowingly heroin or opium addicts. They take "magic medicine" from their local medicine man for their terminal pain, not knowing or caring that it's heroin or opium. There are also some "smoking medicines" that are probably based on marijuana. And so on. And these are not considered evil or rebellious things to do or to consume. It's not like teenagers go to their traditional pharmacist to be rebellious. It's more like their grandmothers go to that guy to get their fix of (unknowingly) heroin, marijuana, and whatever else. It's all "ya," medicine.

So this brings me to the point that drug use of all kinds is pretty rampant in Thai prostitution, but in the context that these kinds of drugs are widely used across Thai society with no real idea that they're evil. For example, marijuana was just a traditional Thai medicine that no one cared to ban nor to glamorize until American soldiers came to Thailand in the 1960s and 1970s and made a big deal of it, and it became strongly classified as an illicit drug, not that grandmothers who smoke it care.

You might know that opium dens flourished in Bangkok also until the American military (Vietnamese war) period, and many of the immigrants from China to Bangkok came firstly for the opium dens. Opium is still smoked by old Chinese-Thai men, but I've never heard of it being something bargirls sit around smoking. Maybe it's popular among the older (over sixty years old sometimes) prostitutes from China you sometimes see in Bangkok's Chinatown, maybe.

Heroin also was the poor or desperate prostitutes' drug of choice until yaba became more popular. My parents would often warn me of the dangers of heroin, since in their generation, it was the big destroyer of finances and families, similar to what yaba is now. My parents had no idea that I would never encounter anyone offering me heroin, but that yaba was everywhere in Bangkok, even outside the massage and hostess and prostitution scene.

And as popular as marijuana is in America, it's not hugely popular with bargirls, nor with young Thai people. They don't like that it makes them hungry and sleepy, something that neither bargirls nor fashionable young people don't like being. It's seen as something for 1960s hippies, the reggae culture (small but not nonexistent in Thailand), and for, as I said, grandmothers trying to relieve their pain.

For regular use, the only drug that's very popular, other than alcohol, is pretty much only yaba. For occasional party use, especially by fashionable young Thai men, ecstasy and cocaine are very popular. Cocaine is seen as a rich people's drug, which I suppose is the same in America. Bargirls themselves are unlikely to be buying cocaine. You might see cocaine being used by rich guys in a hostess club, who then share it with their hostesses. I know that in the hostess club where I worked, there was cocaine being used, but I tried staying as far as possible from it. And of course, some of my coworkers got into sampling their customers' cocaine. As I said, in Thai culture, there's no clear line between illicit drugs and medicinal drugs and mild recreational drugs (alcohol). It's all kind of a blobby mix. So it might be shocking to you that in a high-end hostess club people are sitting around sniffing cocaine, or that Thai grandmothers are swallowing or injecting opium, but it's just a part of the gray-area aspect of Thai culture.

AIDS only happens to bad girls

Thai people believe in karma, and when AIDS first started showing up in Thailand in the 1980s, many people, especially high society people, were sure that this was prostitutes and homosexuals getting what they deserved. What I think is remarkable is not that there is AIDS in the Thai prostitution scene, but that it has not completely swallowed the Thai prostitution scene. Consider that Bangkok is the world center for sex tourism, that many customers insist to go without a condom, and consider that every prostitute is also having sex without a condom with her boyfriend or boyfriends. According to the NGO reports I've read, the rate of HIV infection among bargirls working in the foreigner oriented areas is only around 8-10%. Yes, that's a huge number, but if you compare it with real HIV epidemics in other countries -- even countries not as notorious for prostitution as Thailand is -- it's actually not so bad.

Thai men are not fond of condoms. In general, condoms are considered something you use with a prostitute, or maybe with a one-night stand. A boyfriend doesn't like to use condoms with his girlfriend. If she gets pregnant, she can get an abortion (officially illegal but widely available for poor people, or fly to Singapore or Hong Kong for rich people), or she can just raise the child on her own, but either way, it's not really the boyfriend's concern. Very, very few Thai couples use condoms, unless they are either highly educated or lived in the first world, or perhaps if one of them knows themselves to have some kind of disease (but in my knowledge, couples would just break up at that news, instead of staying together and using condoms).

So however many customers a bargirl has sex with, and however many of those customers don't use condoms -- she very likely is also having sex with some Thai guys, who definitely don't use condoms. And those THai guys are having sex with some other bargirls, and so on and so on.

Until the 1990s, the dislike of condoms extended to prostitution. Thai girls simply didn't know about AIDS and condoms, but the Thai government, along with groups like the United Nations, actually did a remarkably good job of educating prostitutes about condom use. Nowadays, any Thai prostitute, even one fresh from the villages or one working in the worst kind of debt slavery situation, *knows* that condoms are good. That doesn't mean she always uses condoms. But she knows that she should use condoms.

As with other aspects of risk, there's the belief in karma. And Thai bargirls expect themselves to generally have good karma, because they are generally making money to support their parents and offspring, which is definitely a karma-positive thing. And there are ways bargirls protect themselves from bad luck, with visiting certain monks and wearing certain charms. In fact, there are specific amulets sold and worn that are said to provide protection from HIV/AIDS, and many girls believe them to at least have some kind of helping effect.

HIV/AIDS is really rampant among non-prostitutes and the good-time girls who try to have sex with richer men as short-term boyfriends. These girls almost never use condoms. Typically, a girl like this might work as a hotel clerk or a bar server or a tour guide, and have sex with a good number of her foreign male customers, usually expecting shopping trips, and maybe a remote chance of landing a foreign husband -- and always without condoms. It is widely known in Thailand that among these girls, the HIV infection rate is perhaps around 30%. And that's not a scare fact from some Thai grandma. That is verified by international health agencies, who call these kinds of girls "informal sex workers."

And HIV/AIDS is much more prevalent among girls who primarily service Thai men, especially those on the streets. There are two reasons. First, as I said, Thai men dislike to use condoms -- absolutely with girlfriends, and even somewhat with prostitutes, or one-hour girlfriends. The other reason is that girls working on the streets are often girls who aren't allowed to work in the bar or hostess or massage scene because they are widely known to have HIV/AIDS.

Didn't you hear that the bars test their employees for STDs? That's only for show. A "doctor" comes once a month and issues some meaningless cards, and the girls (not the bosses) are supposed to "pay him for testing," about 500 baht each, although he doesn't do any testing, other than signing their certificates, printed in English and Thai, saying the girls don't have any diseases. Or some bars don't even go that far, and let the girls bring their own certificates, which they can usually purchase from internet shops in the bar areas -- printed on the letterhead of any clinic or hospital they want -- for about 50 baht.

But I have to question the usefulness of that kind of testing even if it *were* real. First, as everyone in America knows, HIV can hide in the body without showing up on any tests for a few months. And second, a monthly test only reflects what was true a month ago -- and doesn't tell you if the girl got any diseases since then. All this is is a moot point, because the tests are never done in any serious way, so no matter what, every girl gets a passing grade. I never heard of any girl not getting an automatic "pass" from these "STD checks" that are done just to make the tourist customers feel good.

Sometimes the girls do get a reputation for having HIV, perhaps from an ex-boyfriend who wants to muckrake, or from having obvious physical signs of wasting, or from an angry customer who found himself infected with HIV and is certain he knows which sexual encounter is to blame (you only had sex one time in the past six months, right?). As much as Thai people believe in magic to keep us safe from diseases, we also believe that things like AIDS have a magic all their own, like a ghost spirit, and will jump through any hoops to infect us -- so don't tell us about microbiology, because any Thai person will not want to be anywhere near an HIV/AIDS infected person. Any girl with HIV/AIDS will be forced out of the bar where she works -- unless she is a superstar or there's some other compelling reason -- not so much out of concern for customers, although that is an aspect, as concern for the other girls and management, who definitely don't want to be around an AIDS patient, and who are also afraid that if that girl infects a customer, that customer might come back and infect them.

Life with HIV is bleak in Thailand. Any girl who has it will go to great lengths to hide it. As I mentioned, being known as having HIV will mean being barred not just from work in the sex industry (which actually sounds pretty reasonable to me) but being barred from any kind of employment. It's especially bad for prostitutes, who usually have no family capable of financially supporting them, and no job skills outside of prostitution. The fortunate ones manage to open a shop or other small business and somehow hide their medical condition. The less fortunate ones become complete outcasts. It's like when Thailand used to deal with leprosy a hundred years ago -- the same way it now deals with HIV/AIDS.

Other than AIDS, the other sexual diseases are just about everywhere in the Thai sex industry. They won't kill you and they're not considered a big deal. Most girls get a "small problem" as we call it at least once a month -- meaning an infection of gonorrhea or chlamydia or something similar. We buy some antibiotics from our friends, or get some from our own stash, and the problem goes away soon enough.

Have you heard of herpes and genital warts? Regular people in Thailand really haven't. Or they think it's just some normal "dirt" on their genitals. It's not seen as a disease. I saw a study that said that about 30% of all people in Thailand have genital herpes. That might be true. And the rate among bargirls is definitely higher. I saw many times my coworkers inspecting their genitals and vaginas looking at the bumps and rashes, or worrying slightly about the sores, putting some alcohol on them, believing it's just a minor irritation or rash. They would believe themselves to be STD free even if they were being completely honest with you, because those things are not considered STDs.

We were all "twenty one"

Some Westerners who look with contempt at Thailand and its sex industry imagine that it's mostly a world of foreign pedophiles with twelve-year-old prostitutes. The good news is that child sex tourism, of children that young, exists only deep in the underworld of Thai sex tourism. Yes, it does exist, especially for customers from China, who highly value pre-teen virgins, but it's not in Bangkok, and it's far from the Bangkok sex areas. In fact, most of the "young looking girls" you see with Bangkok sex tourists are around 25-35 years old. Bargirls are much more likely to lie about how young they are (claiming to be younger than their real age) rather than about how old they are (claiming to be older).

In all the venues where I worked, we all told the customers that we're 21 or 22 or 23, maximum. Some girls saying that were 17 while others were in their 30s. Some also had fake ID cards to "prove" their ages. Some even went so far as to have university student ID cards, which are especially popular with Thai customers who like the fantasy of having sex with an innocent university student (kind of the pinnacle of female innocence and desirability in Thai culture!) -- those university cards can be easily bought on the street, or you can just enroll at free Ramkhamhaeng University just to get an ID card. The most common tactic, by far, and one used by all kinds of Thai people, not only bargirls, is to use an older sibling's or other relative's ID card. This is also how young Thai kids sometimes drive cars or motorcycles, using a sibling's license, if they look anything like the sibling. And similarly, 17-year-old bargirls will often "borrow" a 19-year-old sister's ID to prove their ages.

Underage girls, even 17 or so, are no longer common in Bangkok's foreigner-oriented sex bars. This is mostly because Issan is no longer as poor as it used to be, and most girls wait until they're around 18 to start the cycle of getting pregnant and going to Bangkok to support that child. I know that in the bar where I worked on Soi Cowboy, most of the girls were in their late twenties.

However, there *were* two girls who hush-hush admitted that they were 17, and would be legal soon, so it's not such a big deal, to them anyway. Both of them were doing what I said is very commonly done, using a slightly older relative's ID card. This is common throughout the foreigner-oriented bars, such as those on Soi Cowboy.

The age of sexual consent in Thailand is 16 if there's no no prostitution, but 18 for prostitution. (That's confusing to a foreigner, because prostitution is illegal in the first place.) Like most laws in Thailand, this is not really earnestly believed in, but used as a moneymaking opportunity by the police. Girls under 18 working in bars have to pay extra fees to the police, or buy an ID card from them.

And a really big business is getting somebody, usually a Chinese or Japanese tourist who wants young virgins and who somehow angered the wrong people or is otherwise seen as a good target, caught in a "sting" for being with an underage girl. The police don't care about underage girls. Thai policemen themselves often go to prostitutes who are under 18. But they know that this is an especially good moneymaking opportunity.

In fact, in the case of foreigners from first-world countries, those foreigners can face criminal charges back in their own countries if they are publicized as having sex with underage girls -- so the Thai police know that they can make a lot of money in such situations. They can start the negotiations at 10 million baht (about $300,000 USD) -- well how much is it worth it to you to stay out of prison (and not be disowned by your family and society) in your country?

So if you think that the outrage in Thailand is that most prostitutes are thirteen years old or some other such nonsense, your idea has no relationship to fact. But if you think it's an outrage that maybe 5% of the girls in the Western-oriented venues are under 18, and maybe 25% of the girls in the Thai and Japanese or Chinese oriented venues are under 18, then you can be outraged.

Is there realistically anything that can be done about that? It's difficult. You know that the Thai police is only interested in making money. If there was some way for them to make money from actually discouraging or stopping underage prostitutes, instead of profiting from taking hush money from them and selling them fake ID cards, you know that they would do it. And talking or educational campaigns for the girls and their parents are nice, but when your family needs money, are you going to go out and make that money, or listen to a radio advertisement telling you not to be a prostitute if you're under 18?

Now that I've told you

It actually feels great to have put all these things down in writing. I had never seen them written down anywhere, not in Thai nor in English. These facts and observations are passed around among bargirls and sex workers in Bangkok, but even a Thai person not closely associated with the sex trade would not know this. (Actually, a rich Thai person would never believe anything I say, because rich Thai people believe poor people are liars and whiners… but that's a separate story!)

If you're a prospective tourist to Thailand, do these things take away the magic of the bargirl world and experience? I'm sorry if so. I'm not trying to rain on your fun or to prevent you from seeing Thai bargirls and prostitutes. Above all else, Thai bargirls need money -- even if that money goes to their debt or drug handlers -- so I don't know how much you'd be "helping" them by boycotting their line of work.

If you are master of the world, or God, or Buddha reading this, then maybe you can change Thailand so that poor girls are not subject to these things any more. That's not likely, but it's the best I can hope for, since I know that there's really nothing the average reader of this book can do to help what's going on -- other than maybe treating the girls with some understanding and compassion, but well, I'd advocate doing that to anyone, even if they're not in a bad situation in life. That's what Buddhism teaches us, anyway, even if many Thai people don't really follow that teaching.

Prostitution by its nature is going to be ugly wherever you go. Thailand isn't alone. But maybe one big, important difference is I think many foreigners believe that Thailand is different from other countries with prostitution, because back in their home country, prostitution is associated with drugs and debt slavery and STDs and in Thailand it's just happy girls having fun or something like that -- so I wrote this book to tell you that no, Thailand is no different from that situation back in your home country, although Thai people are culturally more likely not to let out the complete truth, especially to a foreign tourist.

Be kind to people around you, and know their situations, and know the consequences of anything you do, that's all I ask.

www.ingramcontent.com/pod-product-compliance
Lightning Source LLC
Chambersburg PA
CBHW062028280526
45787CB00005B/2253